Spurgeon on Adoption

by Charles Haddon Spurgeon

ISBN-13: 978-1985307926

Dear reader,

Thank you for purchasing *Spurgeon on Adoption*. This book contains sermon notes that have blessed millions of believers since their original publication, and The New Christian Classics Library is proud to present them to a new generation of believers.

Care has been taken to preserve the original wording, grammar, and vocabulary of these classic texts (including items that would be considered typos or errors by today's publishing standards). By doing so, modern readers will be able to experience and enjoy these sermons as countless believers have before them.

Our prayer is that you will benefit from and be challenged by the message herein, and we commit you and your reading of this book to our great God who always answers our prayers above and beyond anything we could think or imagine.

Sincerely,

The New Christian Classics Library

For more Christian classics, visit our Facebook page at:

www.facebook.com/thenewchristianclassicslibrary

Table of Contents

ADOPTION

"Having predestinated us unto the adoption of children by Jesus Christ to Himself, according to the good pleasure of His will."

Ephesians 1:5

• • •

It is at once a doctrine of Scripture and of common sense that whatever God does in time He predestined to do in eternity. Some men find fault with divine predestination and challenge the justice of eternal decrees. Now if they remember that predestination is the counterfoil of history as an architectural plan–the carrying out of which we read in the facts that happen–they may perhaps obtain a slight clue to the unreasonableness of their hostility.

I never heard anyone among professors wantonly and willfully find fault with God's dealings, yet I have heard some who would even dare to call in question the equity of His counsels. If the thing itself is right, it must be right that God intended to do the thing. If you find no fault with facts, as you see them in Providence, you have no ground to complain of decrees, as you find them in predestination–for the decrees and the facts are just the counterparts one of the other. Have you any reason to find fault with God that He has been pleased to save you and save me? Then why should you find fault because Scripture says he pre-determined that He would save us?

I cannot see, if the fact itself is agreeable, why the decree should be objectionable. I can see no reason why you should find fault with God's foreordination if you do not find fault with what does actually happen as the effect of it. Let a man but agree to acknowledge an act of Providence and I want to know how he can, except he runs in the very teeth of Providence, find any fault with the predestination or intention that God made concerning that Providence.

Will you blame me for preaching this morning? Suppose you answer, No. Then can you blame me that I formed a resolution last night that I would preach? Will you blame me for preaching on this particular subject? Do, if you please, then and find me guilty for intending to do so. But if you say I am perfectly right in selecting such a subject, how can you say I was not perfectly right in intending to preach upon it? Assuredly you cannot find fault with God's predestination if you do not find fault with the effects that immediately spring from it.

Now we are taught in Scripture, I affirm again, that all things that God chose to do in time were most certainly intended by Him to be done in eternity and He predestined such things should be done. If I am called, I believe God intended before all worlds that I should be called. If in His mercy He has regenerated me I believe that from all eternity He intended to regenerate me. And if in His loving-kindness He shall at last perfect me and carry me to Heaven, I believe it always was His intention to do so. If you cannot find fault with the thing itself that God does, in the name of reason, common sense and Scripture, how dare you find fault with God's intention to do it?

But there are one or two acts of God which, while they certainly are decreed as much as other things, yet they bear such a special relation to God's predestination that it is rather difficult to say whether they were done in eternity or whether they were done in time. Election is one of those things which was done absolutely in eternity. All who were elect, were elect as much in eternity as they are in time. But you may say, Does the like affirmation apply to adoption or justification? My late eminent and now glorified predecessor, Dr. Gill, diligently studying these doctrines said that adoption was the act of God in eternity and that as all believers were elect in eternity, so beyond a doubt they were adopted in eternity.

He further stated that included the doctrine of justification and he said that inasmuch as Jesus Christ was before all worlds justified by His Father and accepted by Him as our representative, therefore all the elect must have been justified in Christ from before all worlds. Now I believe there is a great deal of truth in what he said, though there was a considerable outcry raised against him at the time he first uttered it. However, that being a high and mysterious point, we would have you accept the doctrine that all those who are saved at last were elect in eternity when the means as well as the end were determined.

With regard to adoption I believe we were predestined hereunto in eternity, but I do think there are some points with regard to adoption which will not allow me to consider the act of adoption to have been completed in eternity. For instance, the so close an effect that it really seems to be a part of adoption itself–I believe that this was designed and in fact that it was virtually carried out in God's Everlasting Covenant. I think that it was then actually brought to pass in all its fullness.

So with regard to justification, I must hold that in the moment when Jesus Christ paid my debts, my debts were cancelled–in the hour when He worked out for me a perfect righteousness it was imputed to me and therefore I may as a believer say I was complete in Christ before I was born–accepted in Jesus, even as Levi was blessed in the loins of Abraham by Melchisedek. But I know likewise that justification is described in the Scriptures as passing upon me at the time I believe. "Being justified by faith," I am told, "I have peace with God, through Jesus Christ." I think, therefore that adoption and justification, while they have a very great alliance with eternity and were virtually done then, yet have both of them such a near relation to us in time and such a bearing upon our own personal standing and character that they have also a part and parcel of themselves actually carried out and performed in time in the heart of every believer.

I may be wrong in this exposition. It requires much more time to study this subject than I have been able yet to give to it seeing that my years are not yet many. I shall no doubt by degrees come to the knowledge more fully of such high and mysterious points of Gospel doctrine. But nevertheless, while I find the majority of sound Divines holding that the works of justification and adoption are due in our lives, I see, on the other hand, in Scripture much to lead me to believe that both of them were done in eternity.

And I think the fairest view of the case is that while they were virtually done in eternity, yet both adoption and justification are actually passed upon us in our proper persons, consciences and experiences, in time–so that both the Westminster confession and the idea of Dr. Gill can be proved to be Scriptural. We may hold them both without any prejudice the one to the other.

Well now, Beloved, leaving then the predestination, let us come to as full a consideration as the hour shall enable us to give of the doctrine of "the adoption of children by Jesus Christ to Himself; according to the good pleasure of His will."

First, then, adoption–the grace of God displayed in it. Secondly, adoption–the privileges which it brings. Thirdly, adoption–the duties which it necessarily places upon every adopted child.

First, ADOPTION–THE GRACE OF IT.

Adoption is that act of God whereby men who were by nature the children of wrath, even as others and were of the lost and ruined family of Adam, are from no reason in themselves, but entirely of the pure grace of God, translated out of the evil and black family of Satan and brought actually and virtually into the family of God. They take His name, share the privileges of sorts and they are to all intents and purposes the actual offspring and children of God.

This is an act of pure grace. No man can ever have a right in himself to become adopted. If I had, then I should receive the inheritance in my own right–but inasmuch as I have no right whatever to be a child of God and can by no possibility claim so high a privilege in and of myself, adoption is the pure gratuitous effect of divine grace and of that alone. I could suppose that justification might be by works under the Old Covenant, but I could not suppose adoption to be under the Old Covenant at all. I could imagine a man keeping the law perfectly and being justified by it, if Adam had not fallen. But even upon such a supposition, Adam himself would have had no right to adoption–he would still have been only a servant and not a son.

Above all contradiction and controversy that great and glorious act whereby God makes us of His family and unites us to Jesus Christ as our Covenant Head, so we may be His children–is an act of pure grace. It would have been an act of sovereign grace if God had adopted someone out of the best of families. But in this case he has adopted one who was a child and a rebel. We are by nature the children of one who was convicted of high treason. We are all the heirs and are born into the world the natural heirs of one who sinned against his Maker, who was a rebel against his Lord.

Yet mark this–notwithstanding the evil of our parentage, born of a thief, who stole the fruit from his master's garden–born of a proud traitor, who dared to rebel against his God– notwithstanding all this–God has put us into the family. We can well conceive that when God considered our vile original He might have said within Himself, "How can I put you among the children?" With what gratitude should we remember that though we were of the very lowest original, grace has put us into the number of the Savior's family. Let us give all thanks to the free grace which overlooked the hole of the pit from where we were dug. And which passed over the quarry from where we were hewn and put us among the chosen people of the living God.

If a king should adopt any into his family it would likely be the son of one of his lords–at any rate some child of respectable parentage. He would not take the son of some common felon, or some gypsy child, to adopt him into his family. But God in this case has taken the very worst to be His children. The sons of God all confess that they are the last persons they should ever have dreamed He would have chosen. They say of themselves–

"What was there in us that could merit esteem,
Or give the Creator delight?
Twas 'Even so, Father,' we ever must sing,
'Because it seemed good in Your sight.'"

Again, let us think not only of our original lineage, but of our personal character. He who knows himself will never think that he had much to recommend him to God. In other cases of adoption there usually is some recommendation. A man, when he adopts a child, sometimes is moved thereto by its extraordinary beauty, or at other times by its intelligent manners and winning disposition. But, Beloved, when God passed by the field in which we were lying, He saw no tears in our eyes till He put them there Himself. He saw no contrition in us until He had given us repentance. There was no beauty in us that could induce Him to adopt us—on the contrary we were everything that was repulsive.

And if He had said, when He passed by, "You are cursed, be lost forever," it would have been nothing but what we might have expected from a God who had been so long provoked and whose majesty had been so terribly insulted. But no. He found a rebellious child, a filthy, frightful, ugly child. He took it to His bosom and said, "Black though you are, you are comely in My eyes through My Son Jesus. Unworthy though you are, yet I cover you with His robe and in your Brother's garments I accept you." And taking us, all unholy and unclean, just as we were, He took us to be His—His children—His forever.

I was passing lately by the seat of a nobleman and someone in the railway carriage observed that he had no children and he would give any price in the world if he could find someone who would renounce all claim to any son he might have. The child was never to speak to his parents any more, nor to be acknowledged and this lord would adopt him as his son and leave him the whole of his estates. But he had found great difficulty in procuring any parents who would forswear their relationship and entirely give up their child.

Whether this was correct or not, I cannot tell. But certainly this was not the case with God. His only-Begotten and well-Beloved Son was quite enough for Him. And if He had needed a family, there were the angels and His own Omnipotence was adequate enough to have created a race of beings far superior to us. He stood in no need whatever of any to be His darlings. It was, then, an act of simple, pure, gratuitous grace–and of nothing else–because He will have mercy on whom He will have mercy and because He delights to show the marvelous character of His condescension.

Did you ever think what a high honor it is to be called a son of God? Suppose a judge of the land should have before him some traitor who was about to be condemned to die. Suppose that equity and law demanded that the wretch should shed his blood by some terrible punishment. But suppose it were possible for the judge to step from his throne and to say, "Rebel you are guilty, but I have found out a way whereby I can forgive your rebellions–man, you are pardoned!" There is a flush of joy upon his cheek. "Man, you are made rich! – see, there is wealth!"

Another smile passes over the countenance. "Man, you are made so strong that you shall be able to resist all your enemies!" He rejoices again. "Man," says the judge at last, "you are made a prince! You are adopted into the royal family and you shall one day wear a crown. You are now as much the son of God as you are the son of your own father." You can conceive the poor creature fainting with joy at such a thought, that he whose neck was just ready for the halter should have his head now ready for a crown–that he who expected to be clothed in the felon's garb and taken away to death, is now to be exalted and clothed in robes of honor.

So, Christian, think what you did deserve–robes of shame and infamy–but you are to have those of glory. Are you in God's family now? Well said the poet–

> *"It does not yet appear,*
> *How great we must be made."*

We do not know the greatness of adoption yet. Yes, I believe that even in eternity we shall scarce be able to measure the infinite depth of the love of God in that one blessing of "adoption by Jesus Christ unto Himself, according to the good pleasure of His will." Still, methinks there is someone here who says, "I believe, Sir, that men are adopted because God foresees that they will be holy, righteous and faithful and therefore, doubtless, God adopted them on the foresight of that."

That is an objection I often have to reply to. Suppose, my Friends, you and I should take a journey into the country one day and should meet with a person and should say to him, "Sir, can you tell me why the sails of yonder windmill go round?" He would of course reply, "It is the wind." But, suppose you were to ask him, "What makes the wind?" and he were to reply, "the sails of the windmill," would you not just think that he was an idiot? In the first place, he told you that the wind caused the revolution of the sails and then, afterwards, he tells you that the sails make the wind–that an effect can be the parent of that which is its own cause!

Now, any man you like to ask will say that faith is the gift of God–that good works are God's workmanship. Well, then, what is the cause of good works in a Christian? "Why, grace," they say. Then, how can good works be the cause of grace? By all that is rational, where are your heads? It is too foolish a supposition for any man to reply to without making you laugh and that I do not choose to do. And therefore, I leave it. I say again, Beloved, if the fruits upon a Christian be caused by the root, how can the fruit, in any degree, be the cause of the root? If the good works of any man are given him by grace, how can they, by any pretense whatever, be argued as the reason why God gives him grace?

The fact is we are by nature utterly lost and ruined and there is not a saint in Heaven that would not have been damned and that did not deserve to be damned in the common doom of sinners. The reason why God has made a distinction is a secret to Himself. He had a right to make that distinction if He pleased and He has done it. He has chosen some unto eternal life, to the praise of His glorious grace. He has let others to be punished for their sins, to the praise of His glorious justice and in one as in the other, He has acted quite rightly, for He has a right to do as He wills with His own creatures. Seeing they all deserved to be punished, He has a right to punish them all.

So too, as He has reconciled justice with mercy or mated it with judgment He has a right to forgive and pardon some and to leave the others to be unwashed, unforgiven and unsaved– willfully to follow the error of their ways, to reject Christ, despise His Gospel and ruin their own souls. He that does not agree with that, agrees not with Scripture. I have not to prove it–I have only to preach it. He that quarrels with that, quarrels with God–let him fight his quarrel out himself.

The second thing is, THE PRIVILEGES WHICH COME TO US THROUGH ADOPTION.

For the convenience of my young people–members of the Church–I shall, just for a moment, give you a list of the privileges of adoption as they are to be found in our old Confession of Faith. I know many of you have this book and I am sure most of you will study at home this afternoon if you have opportunity, looking up all the passages. It is the Twelfth Article, upon adoption, where we read–"All those that are justified, God vouchsafed, in and for the sake of His only Son Jesus Christ, to make partakers of the grace of adoption, by which they are taken into the number and enjoy the liberties and privileges of children of God, have His name put upon them, receive the spirit of adoption, have access to the Throne of Grace with boldness, are enabled to cry Abba, Father, are pitied, protected, provided for and chastened by Him as a Father, yet never cast off, but sealed to the day of redemption and inherit the promises as heirs of everlasting salvation."

I shall commence, then, with the privileges of adoption. There is one privilege not mentioned in the Confession which ought to be there. It is this–When a man is adopted into a family and comes thereby under the regime of his new father, he has nothing whatever to do with the old family he has left behind and he is released from subjection to those whom he has left. And so, the moment I am taken out of the family of Satan, the Prince of this world has nothing to do with me as my father and he is no more my father. I am not a son of Satan, I am not a child of wrath. The moment I am taken out of the legal family, I have nothing whatever to do with Hagar.

If Hagar comes to meddle with me, I tell her, "Sarah is my mother, Abraham is my father and, Hagar, you are my servant and I am not yours. You are a bondwoman and I shall not be your bond slave, for you are mine." When the Law comes to a Christian with all its terrible threats and horrible denunciations, the Christian says, "Law! why do you threaten me? I have nothing to do with you. I follow you as my rule, but I will not have you to be my ruler. I take you to be my pattern and mold, because I cannot find a better code of morality and of life, but I am not under you as my condemning curse.

"Sit in your Judgment-seat, O Law and condemn me. I smile on you, for you are not my judge, I am not under your jurisdiction. You have no right to condemn me." If, as the old Divines say, the king of Spain were to condemn an inhabitant of Scotland what would he say? He would say, "Very well, condemn me, if you like, but I am not under your jurisdiction." So, when the Law condemns a saint, the saint says, "If my Father condemns me and chastens me, I bow to Him with filial submission for I have offended Him, but, O Law, I am not under you any longer, I am delivered from you, I will not hear your sentence, nor care about your thunders.

"All you can do against me, go and do it upon Christ. Or, rather, you have done it. If you demand punishment for my sin, look, there stands my Substitute. You are not to seek it at my hands. You charge me with guilt. It is true, I am guilty, but it is equally true my guilt is put upon the Scapegoat's head. I tell you, I am not of your family. I am not to be chastened by you. I will not have a legal chastisement, a legal punishment. I am under the Gospel dispensation now, I am not under you. I am a child of God, not your servant. We have a commandment to obey the Father that we now have. But as to the family with which we were connected, we have nothing to do with it any longer." That is no small privilege–oh that we could rightly

understand it and appreciate it and walk in the liberty
wherewith Christ has made us free!

But now, as the Confession has it, one of the great blessings
which God gives us is that we have His name put upon us. He
will give unto us a new name, as is the promise in the book of
the Revelation. We are to be called after the name of God. Oh,
Remember, Brothers and Sisters, we are men and women, but
we are God's men and women now. We are no longer mere
mortals. We are so in ourselves—but by divine grace we are
chosen immortals—God's sons, taken to Himself. Remember,
Christian, you bear the name of God upon you.

Mark another thing. We have the spirit of children as well as
the name of children. Now, if one man adopts another child
into his family, he cannot give it his own nature, as his own
child would have had. And if that child that he shall adopt
should have been a fool, it may still remain so—he cannot make
it a child worthy of him. But our heavenly Father, when He
comes to carry out adoption, gives us not only the name of
children, but the nature of children, too. He gives us a nature
like His well-Beloved Son Jesus Christ. We had once a nature
like our father Adam after he had sinned. He takes that away
and gives us a nature like Himself as it were "in the image of
God."

He overcomes the old nature and He puts in us the nature of
children. "He sends forth the Spirit of His Son into our hearts,
whereby we cry, Abba, Father." And He gives us the nature
and the character of children, so that we are as much by grace
partakers of the spirit of children of God as we should have
been if we had been His legitimately born children and had not
been adopted into His family. Brethren, adoption secures to us
regeneration. And regeneration secures to us the nature of

children whereby we are not only made children, but are made partakers of the grace of God—so that we are in ourselves made unto God by our new nature as living children, actually and really like Himself.

The next blessing is that being adopted we have access to the Throne. When we come to God's Throne, one thing we ought always to plead is our adoption. The angel that keeps the mercy seat might stop us on the road with saying, "What is your claim to come here? Do you come as a subject, or a servant? If you do, you have no right to come. But if you come as a son, come and welcome." Can you say you are a son in your prayers, Christian? Then never be afraid to pray. So long as you know your sonship you will be sure to get all you want, for you can say, "Father, I ask not as a servant. If I were a servant I should expect Your wages and knowing that as a servant I have been rebellious, I should expect wages of eternal wrath.

"But I am Your son. Though as a servant I have often violated Your rules and may expect Your rod, yet, O Father, sinner though I be in and of myself, I am Your son by adoption and grace. Spurn me not away. Put me not from Your knee. I am Your own child. I plead it. The Spirit bears witness with my Spirit that I am born of God. Father, will You deny Your son?" What? When you plead for your elder Brother's sake, by whom you are God's child, being made an heir with Christ of all things, will He drive away His son? No, Beloved, He will not. He will turn again, He will hear our prayer, He will have mercy upon us. If we are His children we may have access with boldness to the grace wherein we stand and access with confidence unto the Throne of the heavenly grace.

Another blessing is that we are pitied by God. Think of that, children, in all your sufferings and sorrows. "Like as a father pities his children, so the Lord pities them that fear Him." Do you lie sick? The Lord stands by your bedside, pitying you. Are you tempted of Satan? Christ is looking down upon you, feeling in His heart your sighs and your groans. Did you come here this morning with a heavy heart, a desponding spirit? Remember, the loving heart of God sympathizes with you. In His measure, Christ feels afresh what every member bears. He pities you and that pity of God is one of the efforts that flows into your heart by your adoption.

In the next place, He protects you. Just as a hen protects her brood under her feathers from birds of prey that seek their life, so the Lord makes His own loving arms encircle His children. No father will allow his son to die without making some attempt to resist the adversary who would slay him. God will never allow His children to perish while His omnipotence is able to guard them. If once that everlasting arm can be palsied, if once that everlasting hand can become less than Almighty, then you may die. But while your Father lives, your Father's shield shall be your preserver and His strong arm shall be your effectual protection.

Once again, there is provision as well as protection. Every father will take care to the utmost of his ability to provide for his children. So will God. If you are adopted, being predestinated thereunto, most surely will He provide for you—

> *"All needful grace will God bestow,*
> *And crown that grace with glory too;*
> *He gives us all things and withholds*
> *No real good from upright souls."*

Mercies temporal, mercies spiritual you shall have and all because you are God's son, His redeemed child, made so by the blood of Jesus Christ.

And then you shall likewise have education. God will educate all His children till He makes them perfect men in Christ Jesus. He will teach you doctrine after doctrine. He will lead you into all Truth until at last, perfected in all heavenly wisdom, you shall be made fit to join with your fellow-commoners of the great Heaven above.

There is also one thing, perhaps, you sometimes forget which you are sure to have in the course of discipline if you are God's sons and that is God's rod. That is another fruit of adoption. Unless we have the rod we may tremble, fearing that we are not the children of God. God is no foolish father–if He adopts a child, He adopts it that He may be a kind and wise father. And though He does not afflict willingly, nor grieve the children of men for nothing–though when His strokes are felt, His strokes are fewer then our crimes and lighter than our guilt–yet at the same time He never spares the rod. He knows He would ruin His children if He did and therefore He lays it on with no very sparing hand and makes them cry out and groan while they think that He is turned to be their enemy.

But as the Confession beautifully has it, exactly in keeping with Scripture, "Though chastened by God as by a father, yet never cast off, but sealed to the day of redemption, they inherit the promises, as heirs of salvation." It is one great doctrine of Scripture that God cannot, as well as will not, cast off His children. I have often wondered how any persons can see any consistency in Scripture phraseology when they talk about God's people being children of God one day and children of Satan the next. Now, it would startle me not a little if I should step into a lecture room and hear the lecturer asserting that my children might be my children today and his children the next. I should look at him and say, "I don't see that. If they are really mine they are mine. If they are not mine they are not mine, but I do not see how they can be mine today and yours tomorrow."

The fact is that those who preach thus do believe in salvation by works–though they mask and cover it with specious qualifications as much as they may. There is as much need for a Luther to come out against them as there was for him to come out against the Romanists. Ah, Beloved, it is well to know that our standing is not of that character, but if we are children of God nothing can un-child us–though we be beaten and afflicted as children we never shall be punished by being cast out of the family and ceasing to be children. God knows how to keep His own children from sin. He will never give them liberty to do as they please. He will say to them, "I will not kill you–that were an act I could not do–but this rod shall smite you. And you shall be made to groan and cry under the rod"–so that you will hate sin and you will cleave to Him and walk in holiness even to the end.

It is not a licentious doctrine because there is the rod. If there were no rod of chastisement, then it were a daring thing to say that God's children shall go unpunished. They shall, so far as legal penalty is concerned. No judge shall condemn them. But as far as paternal chastisement is concerned they shall not escape. "I have loved you above all the nations of the earth," says God, "and therefore I will punish you for your iniquities."

Lastly, as sure as we are the children of God by adoption we must inherit the promise that pertains to it. "If children, then heirs, heirs of God and joint heirs with Jesus Christ." "If we suffer with Him, we shall also be glorified together."

And now the final point–THERE ARE SOME DUTIES WHICH ARE CONNECTED WITH ADOPTION.

When the believer is adopted into the Lord's family there are many relationships which are broken off–the relationship with old Adam and the Law ceases at once. But then he is under a new Law, the Law of grace–under new rules and under a new Covenant. And now I beg to admonish you of duties, children of God. Because you are God's children it has then become your duty to obey God. A servile spirit you have nothing to do with. You are a child. But inasmuch as you are a child you are bound to obey your Father's faintest wish–the least intimation of His will.

What does He say to you? Does He bid you fulfill such-and-such an ordinance? It is at your peril if you neglect it. Then you are disobeying your Father who tells you to do so. Does He command you to seek the image of Jesus? Seek it. Does He tell you, "Be you perfect, even as your Father which is in Heaven is perfect"? Then not because the Law says so, but because your Father says so, seek after it. Seek to be perfect in love and in holiness. Does He tell you to love one another? Love one another. Not because the Law says, "Love your God," but because Christ says, "If you love Me keep My commandments. And this is the commandment that I give unto you, that you love one another."

Are you told to distribute to the poor and minister unto the necessity of saints? Do it not because you think you are bound by the Law to do it, but do it because Christ says so–because He is your Elder Brother, He is the Master of the household and you think yourself most sweetly bound to obey. Does it say, "Love God with all your heart"? Look at the commandment and say, "Ah, commandment, I will seek to fulfill you. Christ has fulfilled you already—I have no need, therefore, to fulfill you for my salvation, but I will strive to do it because He is my Father now and He has a new claim upon me."

Does He say, "Remember the Sabbath-Day to keep it holy"? I shall remember what Jesus said— "The Sabbath was made for man and not man for the Sabbath," and therefore I shall not be the Sabbath's slave. But as inasmuch as my Father rested on the seventh day, so also will I from all my works and I will have no works of legality to defile His Rest. I will do as many acts of mercy as ever I can. I will seek and strive to serve Him with filial homage. Because my Father rested so will I in the finished work of Christ.

And so with each of the Ten Commandments. Take them out of the Law, put them in the Gospel and then obey them. Do not obey them simply as being the Law graven on tables of stone—obey them as Gospel written on fleshy tables of the heart—"for you are not under the Law, but under grace."

There is another duty, Believer. It is this—if God is your Father and you are His son you are bound to trust Him. Oh, if He were only your Master and you ever so poor a servant you would be bound to trust Him. But when you know that He is your Father, will you ever doubt Him? I may doubt any man in this world. But I do not doubt my father. If he says a thing, if he promises a thing—I know if it is in his power he will do it. And if he states a fact to me, I cannot doubt his word. And yet, O child of God, how often do you mistrust your heavenly Father? Do so no more. Let Him be true. Let every man be a liar—still doubt not your Father. What? Could He tell you an untruth? Would He cheat you?

No, your Father, when He speaks, means what He says. Can you not trust His love? What? Will He let you sink while He is able to keep you afloat? Will He let you starve while His granaries are full? Will He let you die of thirst when His presses burst with new wine? Are the cattle upon a thousand hills His and will He let you lack a meal? Is the earth the Lord's and the fullness thereof and will He let you go away empty and poor and miserable? Oh, surely not! Is all grace His and will He keep it back from you? No, He says to us today, "Son, you are ever with Me and all that I have is yours. Take what you will, it is all your own. But trust to your Father–

> *"Leave to His sovereign will,*
> *To choose and to command.*
> *With wonder filled, you then shall own,*
> *How wise, how strong His hand."*

Now go away, Heirs of Heaven, with light feet and with joy in your countenances. You know that you are His children and that He loves you and will not cast you away. Believe that to His bosom He now presses you–that His heart is full of love to you. Believe that He will provide for you, protect you, sustain you and that He will at last bring you to a glad inheritance when you shall have perfected the years of your pilgrimage and shall be ripe for bliss. "As He has predestinated us unto the adoption of children by Jesus Christ to Himself, according to the good pleasure of His will."

I need not this morning delay you any longer in personally addressing unconverted persons. Their welfare I always seek. I have sought, while speaking to the saints this morning, so to speak that every sinner may learn at least this one fact– salvation is of God alone–and that he may be brought into this state of mind–to feel that if he is saved–God must save him, or else he cannot be saved at all. If any of you acknowledge that Truth, then in God's name I now bid you believe in Jesus. For as surely as ever you can feel that God has a right to save or to destroy you, grace must have made you feel that and therefore you have a right now to come and believe in Jesus. If you know that, you know all that will make you feel empty and therefore you have enough to make you cast your entire hope upon that fullness which is in Jesus Christ.

The Lord bless you and save you! Amen.

ADOPTION—THE SPIRIT AND THE CRY

"And because you are sons, God has sent forth the Spirit of His Son into your hearts, crying, Abba, Father."

Galatians 4:6

• • •

WE do not find the doctrine of the Trinity in Unity set forth in Scripture in formal terms, such as those which are employed in the Athanasian creed, but this Truth of God is continually taken for granted, as if it were a fact well known in the Church of God. If not laid down very often, in so many words, it is everywhere held in solution and it is mentioned incidentally in connection with other Truths of God in a way which renders it quite as distinct as if it were expressed in a set formula. In many passages it is brought before us so prominently that we must be willfully blind if we do not note it. In the present chapter, for instance, we have distinct mention of each of the three Divine Persons. "God," that is the Father, "sent forth the Spirit," that is the Holy Spirit and He is here called, "the Spirit of His Son."

Nor have we the names alone, for each sacred Person is mentioned as acting in the work of our salvation. Look at the fourth verse, "God sent forth His Son." Then note the fifth verse, which speaks of the Son as redeeming them that were under the Law. And then the text itself reveals the Spirit as coming into the hearts of Believers and crying Abba, Father. Now, inasmuch, as you have not only the mention of the separate names, but also certain special operations ascribed to each, it is plain that you have, here, the distinct personality of each.

Neither the Father, the Son, nor the Spirit can be an influence, or a mere form of existence, for each one acts in a Divine manner and with a special sphere and a distinct mode of operation. The error of regarding a certain Divine Person as a mere influence, or emanation, mainly assails the Holy Spirit, but its falseness is seen in the words—"crying, Abba, Father"— an influence could not cry! The act requires a person to perform it. Though we may not understand the wonderful Truth of the undivided Unity and the distinct personality of the Triune Godhead, yet, nevertheless, we see the Truth revealed in the Holy Scriptures and, therefore, we accept it as a matter of faith.

The Divinity of each of these sacred Persons is also to be gathered from the text and its connection. We do not doubt the Divinity of the Father, for He is here distinctly mentioned as "God." Twice is the Father evidently intended when the word, "God," is used. That the Son is God is implied, for though made of a woman, as to His human Nature, He is described as "sent forth" and, therefore, He was preexistent before He was sent forth and made of a woman. This, together with His being called the Son of God and His being spoken of as able to redeem, are, to our minds, sufficient proofs of Deity.

The Spirit is said to do what only God can do, namely, to dwell in the hearts of all Believers. It were not possible for any being to cry in the hearts of a multitude of men if He were not Omnipresent and, therefore, Divine! So here we have the name of each Divine Person, the working of each, the personality of each and, in some degree, the Deity of each within the compass of a few lines. As for Believers in the Lord Jesus Christ, they know how necessary is the co-operation of the entire Trinity to our salvation and they are charmed to see the loving union of all in the work of deliverance. We reverence the Father, without whom we had not been chosen or adopted–the Father who has begotten us again unto a lively hope by the Resurrection of Jesus Christ from the dead.

We love and reverence the Son by whose most precious blood we have been redeemed and with whom we are one in a mystic and everlasting union. And we adore and love the Divine Spirit, for it is by Him that we have been regenerated, illuminated, quickened, preserved and sanctified–and it is through Him that we receive the seal and witness, within our hearts, by which we are assured that we are, indeed, the sons of God. As God said of old, "Let Us make man in Our image, after Our likeness," even so do the Divine Persons take counsel together and all unite in the new creation of the Believer. We must not fail to bless, adore and love each one of the exalted Persons, but we must diligently bow in most humble reverence before the one God–Father, Son, and Holy Spirit. "Glory be to the Father, and to the Son, and to the Holy Spirit; as it was in the beginning, is now, and ever shall be, world without end. Amen."

Having noted this most important fact, let us come to the text itself, hoping to enjoy the doctrine of the Trinity while we are discoursing upon our adoption, in which wonder of Grace they each have a share. Under the teaching of the Divine Spirit may we be drawn into sweet communion with the Father through His Son Jesus Christ, to His Glory and to our benefit. Three things are very clearly set forth in my text–the first is the dignity of Believers–"you are sons." The second is the consequent indwelling of the Holy Spirit–"because you are sons, God has sent forth the Spirit of His Son into your hearts." And the third is the filial cry—crying, "Abba, Father."

First, then, THE DIGNITY OF BELIEVERS. Adoption gives us the rights of children; regeneration gives us the nature of children. We are partakers of both of these, for we are sons. And let us here observe that this sonship is a gift of Grace received by faith. We are not the sons of God by nature in the sense here meant. We are in a sense "the offspring of God" by nature, but this is very different from the sonship here described, which is the peculiar privilege of those who are born again. The Jews claimed to be of the family of God, but as their privileges came to them by the way of their fleshly birth, they are likened to Ishmael, who was born after the flesh, but who was cast out as the son of the bondwoman and compelled to give way to the son of the promise.

We have a sonship which does not come to us by nature, for we are "born not of blood, nor of the will of the flesh, nor of the will of man, but of God." Our sonship comes by promise, by the operation of God as a special gift to a peculiar seed, set apart unto the Lord by His own Sovereign Grace, as Isaac was. This honor and privilege come to us, according to the connection of our text, by faith. Note well the 26th verse of the preceding chapter (Gal. 3:26): "For you are all the children of God by faith in Christ Jesus." As unbelievers we know nothing of adoption. While we are under the Law as self-righteous we know something of servitude, but we know nothing of sonship. It is only after faith has come that we cease to be under the schoolmaster and rise out of our minority to take the privileges of the sons of God.

Faith works in us the spirit of adoption and our consciousness of sonship, in this wise—first, it brings us justification. Verse 24 of the previous chapter says, "The Law was our schoolmaster to bring us unto Christ, that we might be justified by faith." An unjustified man stands in the condition of a criminal, not of a child—his sin is laid to his charge. He is reckoned as unjust and unrighteous as, indeed, he really is and he is, therefore, a rebel against his king and not a child enjoying his father's love. But when faith realizes the cleansing power of the blood of Atonement and lays hold upon the righteousness of God in Christ Jesus, then the justified man becomes a son and a child!

Justification and adoption always go together. "Whom He called, them He also justified" and the calling is a call to the Father's house and to a recognition of sonship. Believing brings forgiveness and justification through our Lord Jesus! It also brings adoption, for it is written, "But as many as received Him, to them gave He power to become the sons of God, even to them that believe on His name." Faith brings us into the realization of our adoption, in the next place, by setting us free from the bondage of the Law. "After that faith is come, we are no longer under a schoolmaster." When we groaned under a sense of sin and were shut up by it as in a prison, we feared that the Law would punish us for our iniquity and our life was made bitter with fear.

Moreover, we strove in our own blind self-sufficient manner to keep that Law and this brought us into yet another bondage which became harder and harder and as failure succeeded to failure we sinned and stumbled more and more to our soul's confusion. But now that faith has come, we see the Law fulfilled in Christ and ourselves justified and accepted in Him—this changes the slave into a child and duty into choice! Now we delight in the Law and, by the power of the Spirit, we walk in holiness to the glory of God. Thus it is that by believing in Christ Jesus we escape from Moses, the taskmaster, and come to Jesus, the Savior. We cease to regard God as an angry Judge and view Him as our loving Father! The system of merit and command, punishment and fear has given way to the rule of Grace, gratitude and love—and this new principle of government is one of the grand privileges of the children of God.

Now, faith is the mark of sonship in all who have it, whoever they may be, for, "you are all the children of God by faith in Christ Jesus" (Gal. 3:26). If you are believing in Jesus, whether you are Jew or Gentile, bond or free, you are a son of God. If you have only believed in Christ of late and have but for the past few weeks been able to rest in His great salvation, yet, Beloved, now are you a child of God! It is not a later privilege, granted to assurance or growth in Grace! It is an early blessing and belongs to him who has the smallest degree of faith and is no more than a baby in Grace. If a man is a Believer in Jesus Christ, his name is in the register of the great family above, "for you are all the children of God by faith in Christ Jesus."

But if you have no faith, no matter what zeal; no matter what works; no matter what knowledge; no matter what pretensions to holiness you may possess, you are nothing and your religion is vain. Without faith in Christ you are as sounding brass and a tinkling cymbal, for without faith it is impossible to please God. Faith then, wherever it is found, is the infallible token of a child of God and its absence is fatal to the claim. This according to the Apostle is further illustrated by our Baptism, for in Baptism, if there is faith in the soul, there is an open putting on of the Lord Jesus Christ. Read the 27th verse: "For as many of you as have been baptized into Christ have put on Christ." In Baptism you professed to be dead to the world and you were, therefore, buried into the name of Jesus. And the meaning of that burial, if it had any right meaning to you, was that you professed yourself to be dead to everything but Christ and henceforth your life was to be in Him and you were to be as one raised from the dead to newness of life.

Of course the outward form means nothing to the unbeliever, but to the man who is in Christ it is a most instructive ordinance. The spirit and essence of the ordinance lie in the soul's entering into the symbol, in the man's knowing not only the baptism into water, but the baptism into the Holy Spirit and into fire—and as many of you as know that inward mystic Baptism into Christ, know also that henceforth you have put on Christ and are covered by Him as a man is by his garment! Henceforth you are one in Christ! You wear His name, you live in Him, you are saved by Him, you are altogether His! Now, if you are one with Christ, since He is a son, you are also sons. If you have put on Christ, God sees you not in yourself but in Christ—and that which belongs to Christ belongs also to you, for if you are Christ's, then are you Abraham's seed and heirs according to the promise.

As the Roman youth, when he came of age, put on the toga and was admitted to the rights of citizenship, so the putting on of Christ is the token of our admission into the position of sons of God. Thus are we actually admitted to the enjoyment of our glorious heritage. Every blessing of the Covenant of Grace belongs to those who are Christ's and every Believer is on that list. Thus, according to the teaching of the passage, we receive adoption by faith as the gift of Grace.

Again, adoption comes to us by redemption. Read the passage which precedes the text—"But when the fullness of the time was come, God sent forth His Son, made of a woman, made under the Law, to redeem them that were under the Law, that we might receive the adoption of sons." Beloved, prize redemption and never listen to teaching which would destroy its meaning or lower its importance! Remember that you were not redeemed with silver and gold, but with the precious blood of Christ as of a lamb without blemish! You were under the Law and subject to its curse, for you had broken it most grievously! And you were subject to its penalty, for it is written, "the soul that sins, it shall die." And yet again, "cursed is everyone that continues not in all things that are written in the Book of the Law to do them."

You were also under the terror of the Law, for you feared its wrath and you were under its irritating power, for often when the commandment came, sin within you revived and you died. But now you are redeemed from all! As the Holy Spirit says, "Christ has redeemed us from the curse of the Law, being made a Curse for us: for it is written, Cursed is everyone that hangs on a tree." Now you are not under the Law, but under Grace, and this because Christ came under the Law and kept it both by His active and His passive obedience, fulfilling all its commands and bearing all its penalty on your behalf! Henceforth you are the redeemed of the Lord and enjoy a liberty which comes by no other way but that of the eternal ransom!

Remember this and whenever you feel most assured that you are a child of God, praise the redeeming blood–whenever your heart beats highest with love to your great Father, bless the "Firstborn among many brethren," who, for your sakes came under the Law, was circumcised, kept the Law in His life and bowed His head to it in His death, honoring and magnifying the Law and making the justice and righteousness of God to be more conspicuous by His life than it would have been by the holiness of all mankind! And He made God's justice to be more fully vindicated by His death than it would have been if all the world of sinners had been cast into Hell! Glory be to our redeeming Lord, by whom we have received the adoption!

Again, we further learn from the passage that we now enjoy the privilege of sonship. According to the run of the passage the Apostle means not only that we are children, but that we are full-grown sons. "Because you are sons" means because the time appointed of the Father is come and you are of age and no longer under tutors and governors. In our minority we are under the schoolmaster, under the regimen of ceremonies, under types, figures, shadows–learning our A B Cs by being convicted of sin. But when faith is come, we are no longer under the schoolmaster but come to a more free condition. Till faith comes we are under tutors and governors, like mere boys. But after faith, we take our rights as sons of God!

The Jewish church of old was under the yoke of the Law. Its sacrifices were continual and its ceremonies endless. New moons and feasts had to be kept. Jubilees had to be observed and pilgrimages made. In fact, the yoke was too heavy for feeble flesh to bear! The Law followed the Israelite into every corner and dealt with him upon every point–it had to do with his garments, his meat, his drink, his bed, his board and everything about him! It treated him like a boy at school who has a rule for everything. Now that faith has come, we are full grown sons and, therefore, we are free from the rules which govern the school of the child. We are under law to Christ, even as the full-grown son is still under the discipline of his father's house, but this is a law of love and not of fear, of Grace and not of bondage.

"Stand fast, therefore, in the liberty with which Christ has made us free, and be not entangled again with the yoke of bondage" Return not to the beggarly elements of a merely outward religion, but keep close to the worship of God in spirit and in truth, for this is the liberty of the children of God! Now, by faith we are no more like bondservants. The Apostle says that, "the heir, as long as he is a child, differs nothing from a servant, though he is lord of all; but is under tutors and governors till the time appointed of the father." But, Beloved, you are now the sons of God and you have come to your majority– you are now free to enjoy the honors and blessings of the Father's house! Rejoice that the free Spirit dwells within you and prompts you to holiness! This is a far superior power to the merely external command and the whip of threats.

Now no more are you in bondage to outward forms, rites and ceremonies, but the Spirit of God teaches you all things and leads you into the inner meaning and substance of the Truth of God. Now, also, says the Apostle, we are heirs–"Why you are no more a servant, but a son; and if a son, then an heir of God through Christ." No man living has ever realized, to the fullest, what this means! Believers are at this moment heirs, but what is the estate? It is God Himself! We are heirs of God! Not only of the promises, of the Covenant engagements and of all the blessings which belong to the chosen seed, but heirs of God Himself! "The Lord is my portion, says my soul." "This God is our God forever and ever." We are not only heirs to God, to all that He gives to His firstborn, but heirs of God, Himself! David said, "The Lord is the portion of my inheritance and of my cup."

As God said to Abraham, "Fear not Abraham, I am your shield and your exceeding great reward," so says He to every man that is born of the Spirit! These are His own words–"I will be to them a God and they shall be to Me a people." Why, then, O Believer, are you poor? All riches are yours! Why, then, are you sorrowful? The ever-blessed God is yours! Why do you tremble? Omnipotence waits to help you! Why do you distrust? His immutability will abide with you even to the end and make His promises steadfast! All things are yours, for Christ is yours and Christ is God's! And though there are some things which at present you cannot actually grasp in your hand, nor even see with your eyes, remember the things which are laid up for you in Heaven, you can enjoy by faith, for, "He has raised us up together and made us sit together in the heavenlies in Christ," "in whom, also, we have obtained an inheritance," so that, "our citizenship is in Heaven."

We enjoy even now the pledge and earnest of Heaven in the indwelling of the Holy Spirit! Oh what privileges belong to those who are the sons of God! Once more upon this point of the Believer's dignity, we are already tasting some of the inevitable consequences of being the sons of God. What are they? One of them is the opposition of the children of the bondwoman. No sooner had the Apostle Paul preached the liberty of the saints, then straightway there arose certain teachers who said, "This will never do! You must be circumcised, you must come under the Law." Their opposition was to Paul a token that he was of the free woman, for behold, the children of the bondwoman singled him out for their virulent opposition!

You shall find, dear Brothers and Sisters, that if you enjoy fellowship with God; if you live in the spirit of adoption; if you are brought near to the Most High so as to be a member of the Divine family, straightway all those who are under bondage to the Law will quarrel with you. Thus says the Apostle, "As then he that was born after the flesh persecuted him that was born after the Spirit, even so it is now." The child of Hagar was found by Sarah to be mocking Isaac, the child of promise. Ishmael would have been glad to have shown his enmity to the bated heir by blows and personal assault, but there was a superior power to check him so that he could get no further than "mocking." So it is now! There have been periods in which the enemies of the Gospel have gone a great deal further than mocking, for they have been able to imprison and burn alive the lovers of the Gospel—but now, thank God—we are under His special protection as to life and limb and liberty and are as safe as Isaac was in Abraham's house.

They can mock us, but they cannot go any further, or else some of us would be publicly hung! But trials of cruel mocking are still to be endured—our words are twisted, our sentiments are misrepresented and all sorts of horrible things are imputed to us—things which we know not! And to all we would reply with Paul, "Am I therefore become your enemy because I tell you the truth?" This is the old way of the Hagarenes—the child after the flesh is still doing his best to mock him that is born after the Spirit. Do not be astonished, nor grieved in the least degree when this happens to any of you! Rather let this turn to the establishment of your confidence and to the confirmation of your faith in Christ Jesus, for He told you of old, "If you were of the world, the world would love his own: but because you are not of the world, but I have chosen you out of the world, therefore the world hates you."

Our second head is THE CONSEQUENT INDWELLING OF THE HOLY SPIRIT IN BELIEVERS—"God has sent forth the Spirit of His Son into your hearts." Here is a Divine act of the Father—the Holy Spirit proceeds from the Father and the Son—and God has sent Him forth into your hearts! If He had only come knocking at your hearts and asked your leave to enter, He had never entered. But when Jehovah sent Him, He made His way without violating your will, but with irresistible power! Where Jehovah sent Him, there He will abide and go no more out forever.

Beloved, I have no time to dwell upon the words, but I want you to turn them over in your thoughts, for they contain a great depth. As surely as God sent His Son into the world to dwell among men, so that His saints beheld His Glory, the "Glory as of the only begotten of the Father, full of Grace and truth," so surely has God sent forth the Spirit to enter into men's hearts, there to take up His residence that in Him, also, the Glory of God may be revealed. Bless and adore the Lord who has sent you such a Visitor as this!

Now, note the style and title under which the Holy Spirit comes to us. He comes as the Spirit of Jesus. The words are "the Spirit of His Son," by which is not meant the Character and disposition of Christ, though that were quite true, for God sends this unto His people, but it means the Holy Spirit! Why, then, is He called the Spirit of His Son, or the Spirit of Jesus? May we not give these reasons? It was by the Holy Spirit that the Human Nature of Christ was born of the Virgin. By the Spirit our Lord was attested at His Baptism when the Holy Spirit descended upon Him like a dove and abode upon Him. In Him the Holy Spirit dwelt without measure, anointing Him for His great work. And by the Spirit He was anointed with the oil of gladness more than His fellows.

The Spirit was also with Him, attesting His ministry by signs and wonders. The Holy Spirit is our Lord's great gift to the Church. It was after His ascension that He bestowed the gifts of Pentecost and the Holy Spirit descended upon the Church to abide with the people of God forever. The Holy Spirit is the Spirit of Christ, because He is Christ's Witness here below, for, "there are three that bear witness on earth, the Spirit, and the water, and the blood." For these and many other reasons He is called "the Spirit of His Son" and it is He who comes to dwell in Believers. I would urge you very solemnly and gratefully to consider the wondrous condescension which is here displayed. God Himself, the Holy Spirit, takes up His residence in Believers!

I never know which is the more wonderful–the Incarnation of Christ or the indwelling of the Holy Spirit! Jesus dwelt here for a while in human flesh untainted by sin–holy, harmless, undefiled and separate from sinners. But the Holy Spirit dwells continually in the hearts of all Believers, though as yet they are imperfect and prone to evil! Year after year, century after century, He still abides in the saints and will do so till the elect are all in Glory! While we adore the Incarnate Son, let us adore, also, the indwelling Spirit whom the Father has sent!

Now notice the place wherein He takes up His residence – "God has sent forth the Spirit of His Son into your hearts." Note that it does not say into your heads or your brains! The Spirit of God, doubtless, illuminates the intellect and guides the judgment–but this is not the commencement nor the main part of His work. He comes chiefly to the affections! He dwells with the heart, for with the heart man believes unto righteousness and "God has sent forth the Spirit of His Son into your hearts." Now, the heart is the center of our being and, therefore, does the Holy Spirit occupy this place of vantage. He comes into the central fortress and universal citadel of our nature and thus takes possession of the whole!

The heart is the vital part. We speak of it as the chief residence of life and, therefore, the Holy Spirit enters it and, as the living God dwells in the living heart, taking possession of the very core and marrow of our being! It is from the heart and through the heart that life is diffused. The blood is sent to the extremities of the body by the pulsing of the heart—and when the Spirit of God takes possession of the affections, He operates upon every power, faculty and member of our entire manhood. Out of the heart are the issues of life and from the affections sanctified by the Holy Spirit all other faculties and powers receive renewal, illumination, sanctification, strengthening and ultimate perfection! This wonderful blessing is ours "because we are sons" and it is filled with marvelous results.

Sonship sealed by the indwelling Spirit brings us peace and joy. It leads to nearness to God and fellowship with Him. It excites trust, love, vehement desire and creates in us reverence, obedience and actual likeness to God. All this and much more, because the Holy Spirit has come to dwell in us! Oh, matchless mystery! Had it not been revealed, it had never been imagined! And now that it is revealed, it would never have been believed if it had not become matter of actual experience to those who are in Christ Jesus! There are many professors who know nothing of this! They listen to us with bewilderment as if we told them an idle tale, for the carnal mind knows not the things that are of God! They are spiritual and can only be spiritually understood!

Those who are not sons, or who only come in as sons under the Law of Nature, like Ishmael, know nothing of this indwelling Spirit and are up in arms at us for daring to claim so great a blessing! Yet it is ours and none can deprive us of it!

Now I come to the third portion of our text—THE FILIAL CRY. This is deeply interesting. I think it will be profitable if your minds enter into it. Where the Holy Spirit enters there is a cry. "God has sent forth the Spirit of His Son, crying, 'Abba,

Father.'" Now notice it is the Spirit of God that cries—a most remarkable fact! Some are inclined to view the expression as a Hebraism and read it, He "makes us to cry," but, Beloved, the text does not say that and we are not at liberty to alter it upon such a pretense! We are always correct in keeping to what God says and here we plainly read of the Spirit in our hearts that He is crying, "Abba, Father."

The Apostle, in Romans 8:15, says, "You have received the Spirit of adoption, whereby we cry, Abba, Father," but here he describes the Spirit, Himself, as crying, "Abba, Father." We are certain that when he ascribed the cry of, "Abba, Father," to us, he did not wish to exclude the Spirit's cry, because in the 26th verse of the famous eighth Chapter of Romans, he says, "Likewise the Spirit also helps our infirmities: for we know not what we should pray for as we ought: but the Spirit itself makes intercession for us with groanings which cannot be uttered." Thus he represents the Spirit Himself as groaning with unutterable groans within the child of God, so that when he wrote to the Romans he had on his mind the same thought which he here expressed to the Galatians—that it is the Spirit, Himself, which cries and groans in us, "Abba, Father."

How is this? Is it not ourselves that cry? Yes, assuredly! And yet the Spirit cries also! The expressions are both correct. The Holy Spirit prompts and inspires the cry. He puts the cry into the heart and mouth of the Believer. It is His cry because He suggests it, approves of it and educates us to it. We would never have cried thus if He had not first taught us the way. As a mother teaches her child to speak, so He puts this cry of, "Abba, Father," into our mouths! Yes, it is He who forms in our hearts the desire after our Father, God, and keeps it there! He is the Spirit of adoption and the Author of adoption's special and significant cry! Not only does He prompt us to cry, but He works in us a sense of need which compels us to cry and also that spirit of confidence which emboldens us to claim such relationship to the great God!

Nor is this all, for He assists us in some mysterious manner so that we are able to pray aright–He puts His Divine energy into us so that we cry, "Abba, Father," in an acceptable manner. There are times when we cannot cry at all and then He cries in us! There are seasons when doubts and fears abound and so suffocate us with their fumes that we cannot even raise a cry– and then the indwelling Spirit represents us, speaks for us and makes intercession for us–crying in our name and making intercession for us according to the will of God! Thus does the cry, "Abba, Father," rise up in our hearts even when we feel as if we could not pray and dare not think ourselves children! Then we may each say, "I live, yet not I, but the Spirit that dwells in me."

On the other hand, at times our soul gives such a sweet assent to the Spirit's cry that it becomes ours, also. But then we more than ever acknowledge the work of the Spirit and still ascribe to Him the blessed cry, "Abba, Father." I want you, now, to notice a very sweet fact about this cry, namely, that it is literally the cry of the Son. God has sent the Spirit of His Son into our hearts and that Spirit cries in us exactly according to the cry of the Son! If you turn to the Gospel of Mark, at the 14 th verse, you will find there what you will not discover in any other Evangelist (for Mark is always the man for the striking points and the memorable words). He records that our Lord prayed in the garden, "Abba, Father, all things are possible unto You; take away this cup from Me: nevertheless not what I will, but what You will." So that this cry in us copies the cry of our Lord to the letter – "Abba, Father."

Now, I dare say you have heard these words, "Abba, Father" explained at considerable length at other times. And if so, you know that the first word is Syrian or Aramaic, or, roughly speaking, Abba is the Hebrew word for, "father." The second word is in Greek and is the Gentile word, "Pater," which also signifies father. It is said that these two words are used to remind us that Jews and Gentiles are one before God. They do remind us of this, but this cannot have been the principal reason for their use. Do you think that when our Lord was in His agony in the garden that He said, "Abba, Father," because Jews and Gentiles are one? Why should He have thought of that doctrine and why need He mention it in prayer to His Father?

Some other reason must have suggested it to Him. It seems to me that our Lord said, "Abba," because it was His native tongue. When a Frenchman prays, if he has learned English, he may ordinarily pray in English, but if ever he falls into an agony he will pray in French, as surely as he prays at all! Our Welsh Brothers and Sisters tell us that there is no language like Welsh–I suppose it is so to them. They will talk English when about their ordinary business and they can pray in English when everything goes comfortably with them, but I am sure that if a Welshman is in a great fervency of prayer, he flies to his Welsh tongue to find full expression. Our Lord, in His agony, used His native language and as born of the seed of Abraham He cries in His own tongue, "Abba."

Even thus, my Brethren, we are prompted by the spirit of adoption to use our own language, the language of the heart– and to speak to the Lord freely in our own tongue. Besides, to my mind, the word, "Abba," is of all words in all languages the most natural word for father. I must try and pronounce it so that you see the natural childishness of it, "Ab-ba," "Ab-ba."

Is it not just what your children say, ab, ab, ba, ba, as soon as they try to talk? It is the sort of word which any child would say, whether Hebrew, or Greek, or French, or English! Therefore, Abba is a word worthy of introduction into all languages! It is truly a child's word and our Master felt, I have no doubt, in His agony, a love for child's words.

Dr. Guthrie, when he was dying, said, "Sing a hymn," but he added, "Sing me one of the children's hymns." When a man comes to die, he wants to be a child, again, and longs for children's hymns. And Our blessed Master in His agony used the children's word, "Abba," and it is equally becoming in the mouth of each one of us. I think this sweet word, "Abba," was chosen to show us that we are to be very natural with God and not stilted and formal. We are to be very affectionate and come close to Him and not merely say, "Pater," which is a cold Greek word, but say, "Abba," which is a warm, natural, loving word– fit for one who is a little child with God and makes bold to lie in His bosom–and look up into His face and talk with holy boldness!

"Abba" is not a word, somehow, but a baby's lisping. Oh, how near we are to God when we can use such a speech! How dear He is to us and dear we are to Him when we may thus address Him, saying, like the great Son, Himself, "Abba, Father." This leads me to observe that this cry in our hearts is exceedingly near and familiar. In the sound of it I have shown you that it is childlike, but the tone and manner of the utterance are equally so. Note that it is a cry. If we obtain audience with a king we do not cry, we speak in measured tones and set phrases. But the Spirit of God breaks down our measured tones and takes away the formality which some hold in great admiration–and He leads us to cry–which is the very reverse of formality and stiffness.

When we cry, we cry, "Abba." Even our very cries are full of the spirit of adoption! A cry is a sound which we are not anxious that every passer-by should hear, yet what child minds his father hearing him cry? So, when our heart is broken and subdued, we do not feel as if we could talk fine language at all, but the Spirit in us sends forth cries and groans! And of these we are not ashamed, nor are we afraid to cry before God. I know some of you think that God will not hear your prayers because you cannot pray grandly like such-and-such a minister. Oh, but the Spirit of His Son cries and you cannot do better than cry, too! Be satisfied to offer to God broken language—words salted with your grief—wet with your tears. Go to Him with holy familiarity and be not afraid to cry in His Presence, "Abba, Father."

But then how earnest it is—for a cry is an intense thing. The word implies fervency. A cry is not a flippant utterance, nor a mere thing of the lips—it comes up from the soul! Has not the Lord taught us to cry to Him in prayer with fervent importunity that will not take a denial? Has He not brought us so near to Him that sometimes we say, "I will not let You go unless You bless me"? Has He not taught us so to pray that His disciples might almost say of us as they did of one of old, "Send her away, for she cries after us." We do cry after Him! Our heart and our flesh cry out for God, for the living God, and this is the cry – "Abba, Father! I must know You! I must taste Your love! I must dwell under Your wings! I must behold Your face! I must feel Your great fatherly heart overflowing and filling my heart with peace!" We cry, "Abba, Father."

I shall close when I notice this, that the most of this crying is kept within the heart and does not come out at the lips. Like Moses we cry when we say not a word. God has sent forth the

Spirit of His Son into our hearts, whereby we cry, "Abba, Father." You know what I mean—it is not alone in your little room, by the old armchair that you cry to God, but you call Him, "Abba, Father," as you go about the streets or work in the shop! The Spirit of His Son is crying, "Abba, Father," when you are in the crowd or at your table among the family! I see it is alleged as a very grave charge against me that I speak as if I were familiar with God. If it is so, I make bold to say that I speak only as I feel! Blessed be my heavenly Father's name, I know I am His child and with whom should a child be familiar but with His father?

O you strangers to the living God, be it known that if this is vile, I purpose to be viler, still, as He shall help me to walk more closely with Him! We feel a deep reverence for our Father in Heaven which bows us to the very dust, but for all that we can say, "truly our fellowship is with the Father and with His Son, Jesus Christ." No stranger can understand the nearness of the Believer's soul to God in Christ Jesus—and because the world cannot understand it, it finds it convenient to sneer—but what of that? Abraham's tenderness to Isaac made Ishmael jealous and caused him to laugh, but Isaac had no cause to be ashamed of being ridiculed since the mocker could not rob him of the Covenant blessing!

Yes, Beloved, the Spirit of God makes you cry, "Abba, Father," but the cry is mainly within your heart and there it is so commonly uttered that it becomes the habit of your soul to be crying to your heavenly Father! The text does not say that He had cried, but the expression is, "crying"—it is a present participle, indicating that He cries every day, "Abba, Father." Go home, my Brothers and Sisters, and live in the spirit of sonship! Wake up in the morning and let your first thought be, "My Father, my Father, be with me this day." Go out into

business and when things perplex you, let that be your resort—
"My Father, help me in this hour of need." When you go to
your home and meet with domestic anxieties, let your cry be,
"Help me, my Father."

When alone, you are not alone because the Father is with you!
And in the midst of the crowd you are not in danger, because
the Father, Himself, loves you! What a blessed word is that—
"The Father Himself loves you"! Go and live as His children!
Take heed that you reverence Him, for if He is a father, where
is His fear? Go and obey Him, for this is right. Be imitators of
God as dear children! Honor Him wherever you are by
adorning His doctrine in all things. Go and live upon Him, for
you shall soon live with Him! Go and rejoice in Him! Go and
cast all your cares upon Him. Go henceforth and whatever
men may see in you may they be compelled to acknowledge
that you are the children of the Highest!

"Blessed are the peacemakers, for they shall be called the
children of God." May you be such henceforth and evermore.
Amen and amen!

THE SPIRIT OF BONDAGE AND ADOPTION

"For you have not received the Spirit of bondage again to fear, but you have received the Spirit of adoption, whereby we cry, Abba, Father. The Spirit, Himself, bears witness with our spirit, that we are the children of God."

Romans 8:15, 16

• • •

THESE two verses are full of the word "spirit," and they are also full of spiritual truth. We have read in previous verses about the flesh and of the result that comes of minding it, namely, death. But now, in this verse, we get away from the flesh and think only of the work of the Holy Spirit upon our spirits–and of the blessed privilege which comes of it – "that we should be called the sons of God." We cannot enter into this except by the power of the Holy Spirit, for the spiritual Truths of God must be spiritually discerned–our eyes need God's Light and our spirits need the Holy Spirit's quickening. We breathe our prayer to the Great Spirit that He would make us feel the full meaning of His Words.

I think that I see in the text the fourfold work of the Spirit. First, the Spirit of bondage. Secondly, the Spirit of adoption. Thirdly, the Spirit of prayer–here it is, "Whereby we cry." And fourthly, the Spirit of witness – "The Spirit itself bears witness with our spirit that we are the children of God."

Consider, first of all, THE SPIRIT OF BONDAGE. Much of the bondage in which we are plunged by our fallen nature is not the work of the Spirit of God at all. Bondage under sin, bondage under the flesh, bondage to the fashions and customs of the world, bondage under the fear of man—this is carnal bondage, the work of the flesh, of sin and of the devil. But there is a sense of bondage to which, I think, the Apostle here mainly alludes, which is of the Spirit of God. Before the Spirit of God within us becomes the Spirit of liberty, He is, first of all, the Spirit of bondage. The Spirit is not, first, a quickening Spirit to us, but a withering Spirit—"The grass withers, the flower fades: because the Spirit of the Lord blows upon it: surely the people is grass."

The Divine Spirit wounds before He heals, He kills before He makes alive. We usually draw a distinction between Law-work and Gospel-work, but Law-work is the work of the Spirit of God and is so far a true Gospel-work that it is a frequent preliminary to the joy and peace of the Gospel. The Law is the needle which draws after it the silken thread of blessing and you cannot get the thread into the stuff without the needle—men do not receive the liberty wherewith Christ makes them free until, first of all, they have felt bondage within their own spirit driving them to cry for liberty to the great Emancipator, the Lord Jesus Christ!

This sense or Spirit of bondage works for our salvation by leading us to cry for mercy. Let us notice that there is a kind of bondage which is, in part, at least, the work of the Spirit of God, although it is often darkened, blackened and made legal in a great measure by other agencies which do not aim at our benefit. That part of the bondage which I shall now describe is altogether the work of the Spirit of God. That is, first, when men are brought into bondage through being convicted of sin.

This bondage is not the work of Nature and certainly never the work of the devil. It is not the work of human oratory, nor of human reason–it is the work of the Spirit of God! As it is written, "When the Spirit of Truth is come, He shall convince the world of sin."

It needs a miracle to make a man know that he is, in very deed, a sinner. He will not admit it. He kicks against it. Even when he confesses the outward transgression, he does not know or feel the inward heinousness of his guilt in his soul so as to be stunned, confounded and humbled by the fact that he is a rebel against his God. Now, no man can ever know a Savior without knowing himself a sinner–even as no man can value a physician while he is ignorant of the existence and evil of disease. By the killing sentence of the Law of God we are bruised, broken and crushed to atoms as to all comeliness and self-righteousness.

This, I say, is the work of the Spirit of God. He works a necessary sense of bondage within us by putting us under a sense of sin. The Spirit of God is always the Spirit of Truth and, therefore, He only convinces men of that which is true. He puts them into no false, or fanciful, or needless bondage. "When the Spirit of Truth is come, He shall convince the world of sin"–because it is sinful. When the Spirit puts men into bondage because they are sinners, He only puts them into their right place. When He came to some of us by the Law, He made us feel what we were by nature–and what we felt and saw was the truth. He made us see things as they really were. Until He came, we put bitter for sweet and sweet for bitter, darkness for light and light for darkness! But when the Spirit of Truth was come, then sin appeared as sin. Then we were in bondage and it was no fancied slavery, but the very truth.

The Spirit of God also brought us farther into bondage when He made us feel the assurance that punishment must follow upon sin, when He made us know that God can by no means clear the guilty and that He was not playing with us when He said, "The soul that sins, it shall die." We were made to feel the sentence of death in ourselves, that we might not trust in ourselves. At that time we trembled on the brink of fate. We wondered that we were not already in Hell. We were so convinced of sin that it was a matter of astonishment to us that the sentence did not immediately take place upon us. We were speechless before God as to excuse or justification. We could not offer anything by which we could turn away the edge of justice, though we saw it like a glittering sword stripped of the scabbard of almighty patience.

Do you know what this means? I can hardly hope that you will prize the Atonement, or feel the sweetness of the expiation by blood, unless, first of all, you have felt that your soul's life was due to God on account of your transgressions! We must know a shutting-up under the sentence of the Law of God, or we shall never rejoice in the liberty which comes to us by Grace through the blood of the Lamb of God! Blessed be the Spirit of God for working in us this double sense of bondage—first making us know that we are guilty and, secondly—making us feel that the justice of God must punish us for sin!

And then, further, the Spirit of God operates as a Spirit of bondage upon the hearts of those whom God will save by bringing them to feel the bitter impossibility of their hoping to clear themselves by the works of the Law. We heard this sentence thundered in our soul – "By the deeds of the Law there shall no flesh be justified in His sight: for by the Law is the knowledge of sin." We could not meet our God under His Law—we looked up to Sinai's fiery summit where the Lord revealed Himself and we felt that its crags were too steep for our tottering feet to climb! Even if the way were smooth, how could we dare to pass through the thick darkness and hold communion with Jehovah, who is a consuming fire?

The Spirit of God once and for all weaned us from all thought of a righteousness of our own. We were divorced from the legal spirit and compelled to abhor the very notion of justifying ourselves in the sight of a pure and holy God by our works, or feelings, or prayers! This was, by His Grace, the work of the Spirit of God! This result is always produced in every child of God, but not always by the same degree of bondage. Fetters of different weights are used in this prison, as wisdom and prudence appoint.

The Spirit of bondage comes not to all alike, for some find peace and life in a moment, and come to Calvary as soon as Sinai begins to thunder. I have known this Spirit of bondage come with great force to men who have been open transgressors. Others who have been kept by the preventing Grace of God from the extremes of open sin have not felt as much of it. But men that have blasphemed God, broken the Sabbath and violated every holy thing–when they are brought before God under a sense of sin–have frequently had a hard time of it. See how Saul was blinded three days and did neither eat nor drink. Read John Bunyan's, "Grace Abounding," and notice the five years of his subjection to this Spirit of bondage.

It must, in Bunyan's case, be noted that his bondage was far from being altogether the work of the Spirit, for much of it arose from his own unbelief. But still, there was in the core and heart of it, a work of the Spirit of God most wonderfully convincing him of sin. I would not wonder if some of my hearers who may have gone far into outward transgression are made to feel, when brought to spiritual life, great grief and humiliation under a sense of their sin. Such bondage often happens to those who, as the old authors used to say, were "close sinners"–men who did not even know that they were sinners at all, but, in consequence of their morality and the strictness of their lives, had a high conceit of their own excellence in the sight of God.

Certain of these people experience most fearful convictions of sin–as if God would say to each one, "I must rid you of your self-righteousness. I must cure you of trusting in your moral life and, therefore, I will let you see into the depths of your depravity. I will discover to you your sins against My Light and knowledge, your sins against conscience, your sins against the Love of God. You are brought into sore bondage, but that bondage shall heal you of your pride." I have noticed one thing more, and that is that those who are, in later life, to be greatly useful are often thus dug, tilled and fed in order that much fruit may be brought forth by them in later years. I have had to deal with as many troubled souls as any living man–and God has greatly used me for their deliverance–but this never could have happened, so far as I can judge, unless I had, myself, been the subject of a terrible Law-work, convincing me not only of my actual sin, but of the source of that sin, namely, a deep and bottomless fountain of depravity in my own nature.

When I have met with persons driven to despair and almost ready to destroy themselves, I have said, "Yes, I understand all that. I have been in those sepulchral chambers and can sympathize with those who are chilled by their damps. I know the heart of a stranger, for I, also, was a captive in Egypt and worked at the brick kilns." In such a case this bondage of spirit becomes a profitable preparation for later work. The sword that has to cut through coats of mail must be annealed in many fires. It must endure processes which a common blade escapes. Do not, therefore, expect that the Spirit of bondage will be seen in all of you to the same degree, for, after all, it is not the Spirit of bondage which is to be desired for its own sake, but that which comes after it–the Spirit of liberty in Christ Jesus!

Our text reminds us that the result of this Spirit of bondage in the soul is fear–"The Spirit of bondage to fear." There are five sorts of fears and it is always well to distinguish between them. There is the natural fear which the creature has of its Creator because of its own insignificance and its Maker's greatness. From that we shall never be altogether delivered, for with holy awe we shall bow before the Divine Majesty, even when we come to be perfect in Heaven. Secondly, there is a carnal fear, that is, the fear of man. May God deliver us from it! May we never cease from duty because we dread the eye of man! Who are you that you should be afraid of a man that shall die? From this cowardice God's Spirit delivers Believers.

The next fear is a servile fear–the fear of a slave towards his master, lest he should be beaten when he has offended. That is a fear which should rightly dwell in every unregenerate heart. Until the slave is turned into a child, he ought to feel that fear which is suitable to his position. By means of this fear, the awakened soul is driven and drawn to Christ and learns the perfect love which casts it out. If servile is not cast out, it leads to a fourth fear, namely, a diabolical fear, for we read of devils, that they "believe and tremble." This is the fear of a malefactor towards the executioner, such a fear as possesses souls that are shut out forever from the light of God's Countenance.

But, fifthly, there is a filial fear which is never cast out of the mind. This is to be cultivated. This is "the fear of the Lord" which is "the beginning of wisdom." This is a precious gift of

Grace – "Blessed is the man that fears the Lord." This makes the saints fearful of offending lest they should grieve Infinite Love. It causes them to walk before the Lord with the fear of a loving child who would not, in anything, displease his parents. When the Spirit of bondage is at work upon the heart, there is much of the fourth form of fear, namely, servile fear– and I tell you that it is the Spirit of Truth which brings this to us because we are in a condition which demands it–we are slaves until Christ sets us free and, being still under the Law, servile fear is our most natural and proper feeling. Would you have the slave rejoice in a liberty which he does not possess? Is he not the more likely to be free if he loathes his slavery? I wish that every man here, who is not a child of God, would become possessed with servile fear and tremble before the Most High!

Now, mark that while this fear lasts, it is intended to work us toward God. I have already touched upon that. This bondage, which causes fear, breaks us off from self-righteousness. It makes us value the righteousness of Christ and it also puts an end to certain sins. Many a man, because he is afraid of the consequences, leaves off this and that which would have ruined him and, so far, the fear is useful to him. And, in later life, the sense of the terror which fear worked in his soul will keep him nearer to his Lord. How can he return to that evil thing which once filled his soul with bitterness and grief?

But now I want to notice that in due time we outgrow this bondage and never receive it again, for, "We have not received the Spirit of bondage again to fear." There comes a time when the Spirit of Truth no longer causes bondage. Why not? Because we are not slaves any longer and, therefore, there is no bondage for us because we are no longer guilty, having been cleared in the court of God and, therefore, no sin should press upon our spirit! We are made to be the children of God and God forbid that God's children should tremble like slaves! No, we have not received the Spirit of bondage again, for the Spirit of God has not brought it to us again. And though the devil tries to bring it, we do not "receive" his goods. And though sometimes the world thinks that we ought to feel it—we are not of the world—and we will not "receive" the world's spirit.

We are new creatures in Christ Jesus! We are not under the Law, but under Grace! And, therefore, we are free from our former bondage. "We have not received the Spirit of bondage again to fear." I know some Christians, or persons who call themselves Christians, who often come under this spirit of bondage. They erroneously say, "If I have sinned I have ceased to be a child of God." That is the spirit of bondage with a vengeance! If a servant disobeys, he will be sent adrift—but you cannot discharge your child. My son is my son forever! Who denies that? Sonship is a settled fact and never can be altered under any possible circumstances. If I am a child of God, who shall separate me from the love of God which is in Christ Jesus, my Lord?

Some perform all religious actions from a principle of fear and they abstain from this and that iniquity because of fear. A child of God does not desire to be thus driven or held back! He works not for reward. He toils not in order to gain salvation. He is saved! And because God has "worked in him to will and to do of his own good pleasure," he, therefore, works out the salvation which God has already worked in! Blessed is the man who knows that he is no longer a servant, but has become an heir of God, a joint-heir with Jesus Christ!

This brings us to our second head which is, THE SPIRIT OF ADOPTION. I should require a week to preach properly upon this blessed theme. Instead of preaching upon it, I will give you hints. Will you kindly notice that the Apostle said, "You have not received the Spirit of bondage"? If he had kept strictly to the language, he would have added, "But you have received the Spirit of"–what? Why of "liberty." That is the opposite of bondage! Yes, but our Apostle is not to be hampered by the rigid rules of composition! He has inserted a far greater word– "You have received the Spirit of adoption."

This leads me to observe that from this mode of putting it, it is clear that the Spirit of adoption is, in the highest sense the Spirit of liberty! If the Son make you free, you shall be free, indeed. If you become sons through that blessed Son, oh, the freeness of your spirits! Your soul has nothing to fear–you need not dread the wrath of God, for He has sworn, "I will not be angry with you, nor rebuke you." The Believer feels the love of God shed abroad within him and, therefore, he exercises a liberty to draw near to God such as he never had before. He has access with boldness! He learns to speak with God as a child speaks with his father! See what a blessed thing is this Spirit of liberty, this Spirit of adoption.

Now, the Apostle said, "You have not received the Spirit of bondage again to fear." What is the opposite of that? He should have added–should he not? – "but you have received the Spirit of liberty by which you have confidence." He has not, in so many words expressed himself thus, but he has said all that and a great deal more by saying, "Whereby we cry, Abba, Father." This is the highest form of confidence that can be thought of–that a child of God should be able, even when he is forced to cry, to cry nothing less than, "Abba, Father." At his lowest, when he is full of sorrow and grief, even in his crying and lamenting, he sticks to, "Abba, Father"! This is a joyous confidence, indeed! Oh, that God may give it to you, dearly Beloved, to the very fullest!

Thus it is clear that the Spirit of adoption is a Spirit of liberty and a Spirit of confidence. As a child is sure that its father will love him, feed him, clothe him, teach him and do all that is good for him, so are we sure that, "No good thing will be withheld from them that walk uprightly." And He will make all things to "work together for good to them that love God." The Spirit of bondage made us fear, but the Spirit of adoption gives us full assurance. That fear which distrusts God–that fear which doubts whether He will remain a loving and merciful God–that fear which makes us think that all His love will come to an end is gone, for we cry, "Abba, Father," and that cry is the death of doubting and fearing!

We sing to brave music, "I know whom I have believed, and am persuaded that He is able to keep that which I have committed unto Him." The Spirit of adoption, moreover, is a spirit of gratitude. Oh, that the Lord should put me among the children! Why should He do this? He did not need children that He should adopt me. The First-born alone was enough to fill the Father's heart throughout eternity! And yet the Lord puts us among the children! Blessed be His name forever and ever! "Behold, what manner of love the Father has bestowed upon us, that we should be called the sons of God!" The Spirit of adoption is a spirit of child-likeness. It is pretty, though sometimes sad, to see how children imitate their parents. How much the little man is like his father! Have you not noticed it? Do you not like to see it, too? You know you do!

Yes, and when God gives the Spirit of adoption, there begins in us, poor fallen creatures as we are, some little likeness to Himself–and that will grow to His perfect image! We cannot become God, but we have the privilege and the power to become the sons of God. "Even to as many as believe on His name" does Jesus give this privilege and, therefore, we grow up into Him in all things, who is our Head—and at the same time the pattern and mirror of what all the children of God are to be! Thus, dear Friends, let us see with great joy that we have not received, again, the Spirit of bondage! We shall not receive Him any more! The Spirit of God will never come to us in that form, again, for now we have been washed in the blood! We have been taken away from being heirs of wrath even as others! We have been placed in the family of the MOST HIGH and we feel the Spirit of adoption within us, whereby we cry, "Abba, Father!"

Just two or three words upon the next office of the Holy Spirit, which is THE SPIRIT OF PRAYER. Whenever the Spirit of adoption enters into a man it sets him praying. He cannot help it. He does not wish to help it—

> *"Prayer is the Christian's vital breath,*
> *The Christian's native air.*
> *His watchword at the gates of death*
> *He enters Heaven with prayer."*

And this praying of the true Believer who has the Spirit of adoption is very earnest praying, for it takes the form of crying. He does not say, "Abba, Father." Anybody can say those words. But he cries, "Abba, Father." Nobody can cry, "Abba, Father," but by the Holy Spirit. When those two words, "Abba, Father," are set to the music of a child's cry, there is more power in them than in all the orations of Demosthenes and Cicero! They are such heavenly sounds as only the twice-born, the true aristocracy of God, can utter, "Abba, Father." They even move the heart of the Eternal!

But it is also very natural praying–for a child to say, "Father," is according to the fitness of things. It is not necessary to send your boys to a Boarding School to teach them to do that. They cry, "Father," soon and often. So, when we are born again, "Our Father, which are in Heaven," is a prayer that is never forced upon us–it rises up naturally within the new-born nature and because we are born-again, we cry, "Abba, Father." When we have lost our Father for a while, we cry after Him in the dark. When He takes the rod to us, we cry, but we cry no other way than this – "Abba, Father, if it is possible, let this cup pass from me."

It seems to me to be not only an earnest cry and a natural cry, but a very appealing cry. It touches your heart when your child says, "Don't hurt me, Father. Dear Father, by your love to me, forgive me." True prayer pleads the fatherhood of God–"My Father, my Father, I am no stranger. I am no foe, I am Your own dear and well-beloved child. Therefore, like as a father pities his children, have pity upon me." The Lord never turns a deaf ear to such pleading. He says, "I do earnestly remember him still," and in love He checks his hand. And what a familiar word it is–"Abba, Father"! They say that slaves were never allowed to call their masters "Abba." That was a word for free-born children only–no man can speak with God as God's children may.

I have heard critics say, sometimes, of our prayers, "How familiar that man is with God." And one adds, "I do not like such boldness." No, you slaves! Of course you cannot speak with God as a child can! And it would not be right that you should! It befits you to fear, crouch and, like miserable sinners, to keep yourselves a long way off from God. Distance is the slave's place–only the child may draw near! But if you are children, then you may say, "Lord, You have had mercy upon me, miserable sinner as I was, and You have cleansed me, and I am Yours. Therefore deal with me according to the riches of Your Grace. My soul delights herself in You, for You are my God and my exceeding joy." Who but a true-born child of God can understand those Words of God–"Delight yourself, also, in the Lord, and He will give you the desires of yours heart"?

I do not know any more delightful expression towards God than to say to Him, "Abba, Father." It is as much as to say – "My heart knows that You are my Father. I am as sure of it as I am sure I am the child of my earthly father! And I am more sure that You would deal more tenderly with me than that my earthly father would." Paul hints at this when he reminds us that our fathers, verily, chastened us after their own pleasure, but the Lord always chastens us for our profit. The heavenly Father's heart is never angry so as to smite in wrath, but in pity, gentleness and tenderness He afflicts His sons and daughters. "You in faithfulness have afflicted me."

See what a blessed state this is to be brought into, to be made children of God, and then in our prayers to be praying, not like serfs and servants, but as children who cry, "Abba, Father"!

Now, the last thing is, THE SPIRIT OF WITNESS–"The Spirit, Himself, bears witness with our spirit, that we are the children of God." There are two witnesses to the adoption of every child of God. Two is a legal number–in the mouth of two witnesses the whole shall be established. The first witness is the man's own spirit. His spirit says, "Yes, yes, yes, I am a child of God! I feel those drawings towards God; I feel that delight in Him; I feel that love to Him; I feel that wish to obey Him which I never would have felt if I were not His child. Moreover, God's own Word declares, 'To as many as received Him'–that is Christ – 'to them gave He power to become the sons of God, even to them that believe on His name.' Now, I have received Christ, and I believe on His name—therefore, I have the evidence of God's written Word that I am one of the sons of God. I have the right, the permission, the authority, to be one of the sons of God! That is the witness of my spirit—I believe and, therefore, I am a child."

Now comes in the witness of the Holy Spirit. Nobody can question His veracity, but how does the Spirit of God witness to our sonship? First, He witnesses it, as I have already said, through the Word of God of which He is the Author. The Word contained in Scripture is quite enough for us if we have a saving faith. We accept it and believe it. The Spirit of God thus witnesses through the Word and that is the surest medium! "We have a more sure Word of testimony," said Peter. That is a wonderful declaration of the Apostle! Peter had spoken about seeing Christ transfigured on the holy mountain. Was not that sure? Yes, it was, but he, in effect, says—We have a more sure Word of testimony than all the sights that we have seen. Therefore we do well if we take heed, as unto a light that shines in a dark place.

Next, the Spirit of God bears witness by His work in us. He works in us that which proves us to be the children of God. And what is that? The first thing is that He works in us great love to God. None love God but those that are born of Him. There is no true love to God in Christ Jesus except in those that have been begotten again by God's own Spirit, so that our love to God is the witness of the Spirit that we are the children of God. Furthermore, He works in us a veneration for God. We fear before Him with a childlike reverence—everything that has to do with God becomes sacred to us when He communes with us. Yes, if He only met us in a dream, we would say, "How wonderful is this place! It is none other than the House of God and the very gate of Heaven."

The place of His feet is glorious in our eyes! The meanest of His chosen are honorable in our esteem! This holy awe of Believers is a proof of their being God's children. If He is their Father, they will reverence Him, for we know that when we had fathers of our flesh, they corrected us and we gave them reverence, for it was due them. Shall we not be in subjection to the Father of our spirits? That subjection is the surest evidence that we are, indeed, the sons of God. In addition to this, the Spirit of God works in us a holy confidence. By His Grace we feel, in days of trouble, that we can rest in God. When we cannot see our way, we go on joyfully without seeing. What is the good of seeing with our own eyes when the eyes of the Lord are running to and fro in the earth to show Himself strong on the behalf of all them that trust in Him?

Our faith feels a joy in believing seeming contradictions; a delight in accepting apparent impossibilities! We have a belief in God's veracity so sure and steadfast that if all the angels in Heaven were to deny the Truth of God, we would laugh them to scorn! He must be true and we know it–every Word in His Bible is as certainly true to us as if we had seen the thing with our own eyes–yes, and truer, still, for eyes deceive and mislead– but God never can! Wherever there is this blessed child-like trust, there is the Spirit's witness that we are the children of God.

And then, again, when the Spirit of God works sanctification in us, that becomes a further witness of our sonship. When He makes us hate sin. When He makes us love everything that is pure and good. When He helps us to conquer ourselves. When He leads us to love our fellow men. When He fashions us like

Christ–this is the witness of the Spirit with our spirit that we are the children of God! Oh, to have more and more of it! Besides which, I believe that there is a voice unheard in the outward ear which drops in silence on the spirit of man and lets him know that he has, indeed, passed from death unto life. This, also, is the seal of the Spirit to the truth our adoption.

Now let us begin at the beginning and bless Him that He has made us feel the bondage of sin. Let us bless Him that He made us fear and tremble–and fly to Jesus. Let us bless Him that He has brought us into the adoption of children. Let us bless Him that He helps us to cry, "Abba, Father." And, lastly, let us bless Him that, tonight, He bears witness with our spirit that we are the children of God!

Dear Friend, do you believe in the Lord Jesus Christ? If so, all the privileges of an heir of God are yours! If you do not believe in Christ, the Spirit of God will never bear witness to a lie and tell you that you are saved when you are not! If you are not saved and not yet a believer in Jesus, I tell you that you are like a blank document to which the Spirit of God will never set His hand and seal, for He is never so unwise as to sign a blank paper! If you have believed, you are a child of God and the Spirit of God sets His seal to your adoption! Go in peace and rejoice in the Lord forever! –

"Nor fret, nor doubt, nor suffer slavish fear–
Your spirit is released, your path is clear!
Let praise fill up your day and evermore
Live to love, to copy and adore!"

Made in the USA
Las Vegas, NV
14 January 2021